Human Data St

CW00927511

Leading Data with the Head and the Heart

Tiankai Feng

Technics Publications
SEDONA, ARIZONA

115 Linda Vista, Sedona, AZ 86336 USA
https://www.TechnicsPub.com

Edited by Sadie Hoberman

Cover design by Lorena Molinari
Author photo by Yan Li.

First Printing 2024

Copyright © 2024 by Tiankai Feng

ISBN, print ed.   9781634625159
ISBN, Kindle ed.   9781634625166
ISBN, PDF ed.   9781634625173

Library of Congress Control Number: 2024941373

Endorsements

Tiankai Feng is a creative force of nature in the data space. Since bursting onto the scene with his "Governors of Data" rap song and music parodies, he has proven time and again that he can effectively wrap the truth about data management in a business-accessible coating. His new book, Humanizing Data Strategy, is a natural extension of his unique form of thought leadership.

Tiankai strives to illuminate the human side of data strategy. By acknowledging the inherent biases and emotional influences in data analysis, he underscores the need for empathy and compassion in the realm of data-driven decision-making. With his trademark blend of personal anecdotes and professional wisdom, he offers a simple but compelling 5Cs framework for making data strategy more inclusive and impactful. A must-read for anyone looking to humanize their data practices and foster a more collaborative and ethical data culture at their enterprise.

Scott Taylor – The Data Whisperer,
Author of *Telling Your Data Story*

In an era where books come and go, this book by Tiankai Feng stands out! From the very first page, it's clear that this book is both thoughtful and heartfelt in a world where reason and logic have sanitized our senses, and data rules the world. Tiankai offers readers a deep well of wisdom, along with meaningful reflection on the subject of all things data. His perspective, thought leadership, and unique way of humanizing the entire lifecycle is refreshing. I highly recommend this book to data nerds, strategists, book snobs, and literary aficionados alike.

Sol Rashidi
Bestselling author of *Your AI Survival Guide*, Former Chief
Data/Analytics/AI Officer @ Fortune 100s,
Forbes 'AI Visionary of the 21st Century'

Too often, we relegate people to a workstream. In his book "Humanizing Data Strategy," author Tiankai Feng helps us understand that the "people" part of a data strategy is our superpower. From the 5Cs Framework to the roles we all play, Feng breaks down how to build a killer data strategy in your own organization. A must read for anyone starting (or re-starting) their data strategy.

Laura Madsen, Author of *AI and the Data Revolution*

Humanizing Data Strategy brilliantly bridges the gap between data-driven insights and human-centric decision-making. This book is a must-read for any data professional looking to balance technical expertise with the essential human touch.

Robert S. Seiner
President & Principal of KIK Consulting & Educational Services

As the founder of a data community and education company, I encounter an endless amount of literature and content on data strategy, but 'Humanizing Data Strategy' stands out as a true game-changer. This book brilliantly bridges the gap between data expertise and human-centric approaches, a balance so many data leaders try to achieve.

Whether you're working at a startup or a Fortune 500 company, this book will reshape how you approach data governance and focus on the soft skills needed to bring your program to the next level.

Philip Black
CEO and Founder: DataQG

"Humanizing Data Strategy" is a resource for anyone involved in data management, from seasoned professionals to those just starting out. It is a must-read for anyone looking to enhance their data strategy with a people-first approach that drives real, sustainable success.

George Firican, Founder of LightsOnData, and
Data Governance instructor and expert

Data problems are people problems, and this book eloquently addresses the real issue — people and their attitude/approach towards data. But what really moved me was reading a reference to a data scientist as "she". I felt seen and heard, this is such a great step forward inclusion and inspiring young girls and women. Thank you.

Susan Walsh
Founder & MD, The Classification Guru

Humanizing Data Strategy is a must read for data practitioners and techies of all stripes, forcing you to rethink your data relations, putting your customers, those you serve, and human factors at the center from the start; one data conversation, humanity transformed, at a time!

Pedro Cardoso, known as "the Data Ninja", is a Data & AI thought leader and is Global Director, Data Strategy @ Syniti

The human side of data is the key to succeed with data strategies. However objective and technical data may appear, at some point, a human was involved. Remembering this is the key.

Ole Olesen-Bagneux
Author of ***The Enterprise Data Catalog***

To Sky and Cloud—one day you'll understand.

Acknowledgments

I always liked working in data and sharing my experiences and insights with others. Being able to write a book about my favorite aspect of data–the people aspect–is truly a dream come true. Getting here didn't just happen by accident. I am very lucky that I had people around me who always supported and encouraged me to continue. I want to say a heartfelt thank you to all of them.

To my wife, Yan Li, and my two sons, Sky and Cloud, I could have never made it this far without your love and support. I promise I will make it up to you for all the evenings and weekends I spent writing this book instead of being with you.

To my parents, Dr. Lu Tian and Dr. Kuiyuan Feng, you always wanted me to get a Ph.D. to become a known, published expert. Guess what? I am a known data expert and published this book, and I didn't need a Ph.D. to do it after all.

To my lifelong friends Adam Janisch, Hen-Ju Sophia Song, Magnus Kalass, and Jan Werner–we learned together and became adults together, and now I want to share this biggest achievement of my adult life so far with you as well. Thanks for your friendship and for letting me realize that being myself is truly being the best version of me.

To my childhood piano teacher, Jutta Dobbertin, you always encouraged me to be disciplined in practicing the piano and to stay true to my creativity. Combining my musical talents with my passion for data has brought me here. I'm an author now!

To my previous managers and leaders, Lars-Alexander Mayer, Andreea Niculcea, Blake Stonebanks, Jacques Ohannessian, Jasmin Herrmann, Jonathan Cavalier, and Michelle Robertson, you have all always pushed me to be better and more impactful. I would not have had the confidence to write this book without your support.

To my previous colleagues turned friends, Christopher Lewis, Dr. Jun-Seo Lee, Robert Farouk-Butze, Krys Burnette, Adrian Sennewald, Jana Nübler, Agnieszka Chruszczow, Chris Brown, and Petra Lehoczky: we worked together, laughed together, and went through good and bad times together, but most importantly you were there for me, especially during a difficult time when I needed you the most (IYKYK). You are the reason I kept my strength and optimism to be able to write this book.

To my current colleagues Emily Gorcenski, Kelsey Beyer, Javier Molina Sanchez, and Lauris Jullien, thank you for all the great collaboration at Thoughtworks, where I can truly be myself and be valued for my value-driven people-first approaches.

To my DAMA Germany friends Frank Pörschmann, Ekkehard Schwarz, Christian Hädrich, and Karen Gärtner, I am truly honored to build a data management community in Germany with you, and there are so many more great things coming.

To my fellow thought leaders and respected experts Laura Madsen, Robert S. Seiner, Scott Taylor, Nicola Askham,

Katharine Jarmul, Ole Olesen-Bagneux, Philip Black, Susan Walsh, George Firican, and Pedro Cardoso, I am inspired by your knowledge, content, and personalities every day.

To Bilge Gizem Yakut, thank you for always believing in my leadership and my expertise, and for encouraging me to write a book before I even had the opportunity.

To Steve Hoberman, thanks for this one-in-a-lifetime opportunity to publish a book.

Contents

Foreword

It is an honor and a privilege to write this foreword for a book that promises to transform how we think about data strategy. "Humanizing Data Strategy: Leading Data with the Head and the Heart," written by my friend and former colleague Tiankai Feng, is a profound exploration of the intersection between data and human experience.

I clearly remember our first in-person interaction a couple of years ago over lunch. During our conversation, I shared my observation that Tiankai, with his remarkable aptitude and insight, seemed destined for a career in data governance. His enthusiasm and curiosity were palpable, and he embraced the idea with open arms. It has been astonishing to witness his journey since then, as he navigates the complexities of data with ingenuity.

Tiankai has always had a unique ability to embrace change and challenge. His methods extend far beyond the visible, such as conference speaking and online videos. Tiankai truly connects with people, easing them into topics that are often outside their comfort zones. This talent is evident in his approach to data, which he tackles not just with technical expertise but with a genuine human touch.

In today's world, data is becoming increasingly crucial. In other words, it is a very important and often underutilized asset. Many readers of this book have experienced firsthand the evolution of technology from a mere support function into a core backbone for many organizations. This journey has taken many years and is still ongoing in certain areas. However, the transformation in awareness regarding the importance of data—its structure and the impact of having a fit-for-purpose data strategy—began later but is progressing at an exponential rate. New technical capabilities offer exhilarating new opportunities for data. The difference between having a good data strategy and neglecting one is profound. Organizations with a well-defined data strategy can harness data to drive innovation, enhance decision-making, and gain a competitive edge. They are able to anticipate market trends, personalize customer experiences, and improve operational efficiency. Conversely, those without a solid data strategy often struggle with data silos, poor data quality, and missed opportunities, leading to inefficiencies, increased risks, and a reactive rather than proactive approach to challenges.

Had I received this book without knowing its author, I would have immediately suspected Tiankai's involvement. His voice resonates throughout, creating connections with readers on a personal level and making complex topics approachable. When you think about data, human connection might not be the first thing that comes to mind, but Tiankai challenges this notion brilliantly.

This book is a blend of personal stories and theoretical insights, guiding you towards and through the framework of the five Cs:

- **Competence**: Empowering everyone with the right knowledge across business, data, and technological expertise, fostering leadership and confidence by addressing intrinsic motivations of learning, growth, and human connection. This leads to a more robust data culture.

- **Collaboration**: Igniting inter- and cross-functional collaboration through transparency, accountability, and shared goals. Tiankai advocates for ways of working that emphasize problem-solving, experimentation, and embracing subjectivity rather than forcing artificial objectivity.

- **Communication**: Utilizing communication methods that focus on audience-specific narratives, expressing undeniable business value and personal reward, and providing continuous impulses for proactive and reactive contributions to make data efforts successful.

- **Creativity**: Providing the motivation, environment, and reward for both proactive and reactive creativity, leading to continuous improvements and innovations in data operations and technologies.

- **Conscience**: Applying critical thinking and human judgment through cross-functional decision-making bodies to ensure data efforts remain secure, compliant, and ethical.

Tiankai Feng's professional journey is a testament to his dedication and expertise. With extensive experience handling various data assets—from e-commerce data and consumer insights to product data in a multinational context—he has seen data at its full potential on both small and large scales. Tiankai has navigated the complexities of data within multinational companies, coordinating multiple departments and leveraging data insights to drive smart decision-making at the senior management level. His innovative ideas and commitment to connecting with people on a human level set him apart as both a leader and a visionary thinker. Now, in his consulting role, Tiankai is perfectly positioned to share his wealth of experience and solution-oriented approach with companies across different industries. He supports these organizations in developing scalable data solutions, enabling them to harness their data's full potential and drive meaningful, data-informed transformations.

The structure of this book is meticulously designed to guide readers through a comprehensive understanding of data strategy. Each section builds upon the previous one, creating a cohesive and engaging narrative. Readers can expect to gain both practical insights and theoretical knowledge, making this book a valuable resource for anyone interested in data.

In a world where data's importance continues to grow, this book is timely and relevant. Tiankai addresses the current trends and challenges, offering solutions and perspectives that are both innovative and practical. His unique approach, blending technical expertise with a human touch, provides readers with a fresh and necessary perspective on data strategy.

As you read this book, you will not only learn from Tiankai's expertise but also feel his genuine passion for connecting with people and making complex topics accessible. This blend of personal stories and professional insights will inspire and empower you to approach data with both the head and the heart.

I invite you to dive into "Humanizing Data Strategy" and apply its lessons to your work and life. Tiankai Feng's wisdom and guidance will undoubtedly lead you to a deeper understanding of data and its potential. Are you ready to embark on this journey?

Jasmin Herrmann
Senior IT Risk, Compliance, Governance, and Security Executive specializing in Transformation Projects and Strategic Initiatives in Multinational Companies

Introduction

Every one of us is human. You, the reader, our clients and stakeholders, our vendors and partners, our coworkers and collaborators, and, most importantly, the customers whose data we attempt to analyze, are all human beings.

We try to be analytical, reasonable, and fact-based ("data-driven"), but the truth is that we're all emotional, irrational, and unpredictable. It is, quite simply, impossible to create an impartial and objective truth. Yet, we frequently portray data and analytics as serving the sole purpose of "fact-based decision-making" and presenting data as the final and inarguable truth.

From the decisions made during data collection to those made during processing, transforming, consuming, and interpreting, human decisions introduce bias into data at every stage of its lifecycle. Machine learning and artificial intelligence, along with other cutting-edge technologies, only serve to amplify our bias and speed up the application of our biased conclusions to data while making them less transparent.

Furthermore, human factors frequently render our methods of leading, managing, and directing data teams and functions inefficient. Rather than addressing the underlying causes, we hastily conclude that additional reorganization or a change in top leadership is necessary.

The legendary human rights activist Maya Angelou once said: "I've learned that people will forget what you said, people will forget what you did, but people will never forget how you made them feel." Considering everyone you've worked with so far, you'll see this is true. You're more likely to characterize their attitude and personality than any particular words or actions they may have taken.

Consequently, we should stop viewing the "people" component of data strategy as a potential weak spot and start incorporating human qualities like empathy, compassion, and understanding of human motives into the mix.

Data is more popular than ever because:

- Digital transformation has escalated, increasing the speed and complexity of data projects.

- The advancements in data literacy and data democratization have enabled individuals organization-wide to utilize data to create interesting new projects, but this has resulted in a growing lack of transparency of data usage.

- Governmental organizations are beginning to acknowledge the dangers associated with artificial intelligence and are targeting businesses with rules and legislation.

- Significant advancements in emerging technologies, such as artificial intelligence and cloud storage, have made data processing more powerful than ever.

All of it suggests that handling data should be done more deliberately, organized, and securely. Put another way, we need a data strategy that reduces risks while maximizing the benefits of collecting, analyzing, and using data.

People, process, and technology all need to work together for a data strategy to be effective. However, dealing with people is the hardest yet most rewarding part. From personal experience, I can tell that getting a bunch of people to work together toward the same objective is more fulfilling than releasing a new dashboard.

Everyone is special in their own way, molded by the unique combination of our family history, upbringing, and life experiences.

I was born in Germany as a child of two Chinese immigrants who both came to Germany to do their Ph.D. in engineering and then decided to stay permanently. When growing up, I was often the only Asian face in school or any community and I became an extrovert, loud and humorous to break stereotypes around Asian people and to be more easily included.

All my childhood (and still even now as an adult, really), I had an identity crisis between being German or Chinese. Not only did I constantly get asked if I felt more like a Chinese or like a German, I often was judged by "the other identity." If I wasn't on time, I wasn't German enough. If I wasn't great in playing table tennis, I wasn't Chinese enough. It made me feel like a foreigner, no matter where I was. I got used to feeling different, but I also took that as a motivation to adapt to and connect with others. Simultaneously, I followed my parents' guidance: to succeed in life, I needed to succeed in school, and so I always got excellent grades in math and science classes.

Why am I telling you all of this? Three reasons:

1. Our experiences make us all unique, and using a one-size-fits-all approach to guide people is not going to work

2. We know from our own identities that not everything is black and white, so even in data we need to acknowledge that

3. My own experiences led me to have a strong passion for making data a more inclusive and fulfilling area to work in–and this book should enable and inspire that.

So, in this book–I want you as a reader to take away the following things:

- Decode the key areas to make a data strategy more "human"

- Think more about the human factors in your day-to-day

- Apply a framework to assess and improve your data strategy

Are you ready to dive into the "people" side of data strategy? Buckle up, let's begin!

One

5Cs Framework

I wanted to start this chapter with something smart about the definition of data strategy, and after some research, I realized there is no consensus about what it is. The definitions do have some things in common: long-term planning, people, process, technologies, and managing information and data.

Taking a more strategic approach to managing all data initiatives is necessary, in my opinion, because every day, all businesses generate, gather, process, and use vast amounts of data. So, here is how I define a data strategy:

Data strategy is a long-term plan that defines the people, processes, and technologies to create, process, and use data to intentionally drive value in a meaningful, secure, and transparent way.

So far so good, but there are, in my experience, also five main reasons why data strategies fail:

1. Data literacy has not been enough of a focus, leading to many people just not "adopting" data work in their day-to-day

2. Data efforts have not solved the siloed way of working and might have even made things worse by dividing into factions of "I like data" versus "I don't like data"

3. Nobody understands what and why data needs to be treated as an asset, so just out of frustration of not knowing what to do, people don't engage

4. Data is seen and operated as a chore, and it is treated as a monotonous, tedious way of working

5. Data has led to a few too many big issues that escalated to the top leadership level (keyword "POLITICS!"), and now, just talking about it feels like a minefield

So, to make the human aspect of data strategy understood and memorable, but also actionable by solving the issues I mentioned above, I broke the "people side" of data strategy into five dimensions. These dimensions are the "5 Cs":

1. **Competence:** Empowering everyone with the right knowledge across business, data, and technological expertise by addressing the intrinsic motivations of learning, growing, and the human connection, leading to an improved data culture.

2. **Collaboration:** Igniting inter- and cross-functional collaboration through transparency, accountability, and sharing goals, as well as implementing ways of

working that focus on problem-solving, experimentation, and embracing subjectivity instead of forcing artificial objectivity.

3. **Communication:** Using methods of communication that focus on audience-specific narrative structures, expressing undeniable business value and personal reward, and providing continuous impulses for proactive and reactive contributions to make data efforts successful.

4. **Creativity:** Providing the motivation, environment, and reward for proactive and reactive creativity, leading to continuous improvements and innovations around data operations and technologies.

5. **Conscience:** Applying critical thinking and human judgment through cross-functional decision-making bodies to keep data efforts secure, compliant, and ethical.

You might ask: "But wait—you are diving deeper into the people part of data strategy, but what about the process and technology aspects?" Well, the people aspect I am describing also has implications on process and technology.

We still need humans to oversee anything having to do with data, even though automation has come a long way. This is because we still don't have sufficient trust in machines to replace human critical thinking. This holds true for any business process or data-specific process. The following chapters will go into great detail, and they will undoubtedly touch on processes and the part humans play in them.

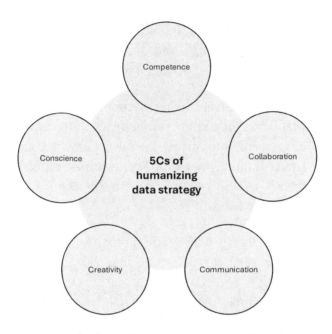

When it comes to technology, my firm belief is that every technology is a tool. Despite what some vendors and providers may say, their purpose is not to substitute humans but to facilitate their work and help them achieve their goals. Data discovery and obtaining clearance for data change requests are two examples of less common but extremely time-consuming jobs that fall under this category. It's still applicable to routine and repetitive laborious chores, but it can now be expanded to include these as well. Tech terms like "user experience," "collaborative features," and "AI-empowered automation" often refer to the human element. It would be fantastic if these encompassed the ability to enable and support the human side of data that I'm outlining here.

In the following chapters, we will delve deeper into these five elements, providing examples and practical help along the way.

Two

Competence

You may have heard, "I'm not an expert in this, but..." at some point in your life. Being termed an "expert" indicates that there is nothing more to learn. Yet, I actually see this as a lovely indication that somebody has learned and acknowledged this fundamental principle, humbleness, and modesty, in contrast to what others hear.

But it's hard to do that in the data world, which is both extremely varied and growing at a dizzying rate. Expressing your lack of expertise in a particular area and providing a solution based on your knowledge and experience demonstrates a healthy degree of confidence. It also indicates that you aren't scared to communicate your thoughts without being afraid of counter-opinions, which are often a wonderful way to learn and grow.

This is what competence in data strategy really is all about—continuous learning and confidence to act while being able to recognize and admit your limits to let the more knowledgeable either make the decision or help you make the right decision.

The basic implication is to make the most of data by exploiting and reusing it for better decision-making, since data should be seen as an asset. But the sort of decision to make and the availability of data determine the extent to which "improved decision-making" may occur.

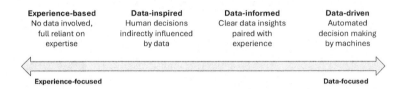

In my view, there are four types of decision-making with an increasing level of influence of data:

- **Experience-based:** Decisions are completely based on experience and expertise. Often referred to as "gut feeling decisions" as well, we should not underestimate human intuition and reflexes. *Example: Go to market strategy of a brand new disruptive product*

- **Data-inspired:** Decisions that are indirectly influenced by data. There are no direct insights related to the decision to make, but someone inferred from other insights what the right choice for a decision might be. *Example: Becoming an early adopter for a new sales channel with low empirical data*

- **Data-informed:** Decisions are made with the acknowledgment of directly related insights from the data. Facts are balanced with human expertise to make the right decision. *Example: Launching a marketing campaign that was informed by previous similar campaign insights*

- **Data-driven:** Decisions are completely automated based on data-based rules, and no human oversight is involved anymore. *Example: Dynamic pricing on eCommerce.*

The overarching goal of a data strategy should be to increase data's impact on human decision-making. Nevertheless, data will never fully replace human critical thinking. Rather, it will play an enabling role. The most important thing is to strike a balance and be deliberate about your judgments, both now and in the future.

Data literacy versus business acumen

Over the last few years, one buzzword has emerged and has steadily increased in importance: data literacy. Data literacy is "the ability to read, work with, analyze and communicate with data."[1]

---

[1]Morrow, J. (2021). Be Data Literate: The Data Literacy Skills Everyone Needs to Succeed. India: KoganPage.

Equipping an entire organization with a basic understanding of how data works and how to work with data is a great, continuous effort. Still, from my point of view, it feels a little one-sided and, to be frank, a little pretentious towards non-data professionals. If all employees and subject matter experts should take a step toward data via learning and growth, shouldn't data professionals do the same towards business expertise?

Hence, I don't think training everyone on data literacy is enough. We must invest equally in business acumen for the continuously changing and evolving roles of data professionals in an organization.

If we follow the trend of decentralizing data efforts through empowered business areas owning and being accountable for their value-creation with data, then having data literacy and business acumen is more important than ever, and we must recognize that.

What should be the scope of data literacy and business acumen, then? As Ridsdale et al.[2] defined it, there are five key knowledge areas within data literacy: conceptual framework, data collection, data management, data evaluation, and data application.

The further you go through the data lifecycle and into domains specific to your organization, the more contextual and sensitive it becomes. This means you cannot outsource data literacy and business acumen efforts, at least not

---

[2] Ridsdale, Chantel, et al. "Strategies and best practices for data literacy education: Knowledge synthesis report." (2015).

completely. However, executing all upskilling and learning efforts through internal resources is also a big cost commitment, and not every company has the financial flexibility to do so.

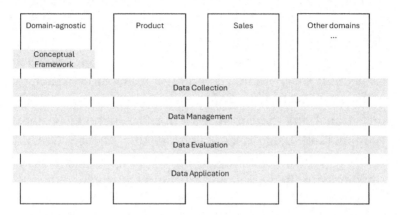

Consequently, the most effective, efficient, and scalable plan would involve combining in-house attempts to demonstrate the practical application of theoretical concepts with external offerings of live, interactive sessions and on-demand learning materials. This would result in an approach that is both engaging and informative, and it would also save money.

Having a "humanized" data strategy means investing consciously in the growth and competencies of everyone who contributes to making data valuable. This includes increasing business acumen for data professionals and data literacy for collaborators in other functions.

Hoping for everyone to just proactively learn what's needed is not enough—simply because not everyone feels empowered to use their working hours to "learn" rather than "do," and even if they do learn, they might not learn what's really needed to make the data strategy a successful endeavor.

For example, when a data analyst who creates a Power BI dashboard is learning about what decisions corporate treasury is making, but the key stakeholder in Controlling decides to learn more about how to code machine learning models in Python—then they are both upskilled in their respective areas of choice. Still, it doesn't directly help to make the dashboard more adopted or valuable. A more intentional and synchronized effort to increase business acumen and data literacy within the finance domain, defined in the data strategy, could have aligned content and timeliness of the upskilling and could have helped directly with their collaboration.

From theory to practice—or how not to forget

Learning new skills and knowledge is great, but if we don't apply the learned theory in practice, then we can quickly forget it again. According to the "Forgetting Curve," established by German psychologist Hermann Ebbinghaus in the 1800s, we forget 90% of all new information within a week—unless we reinforce what we learned.[3]

---

[3] https://www.ncbi.nlm.nih.gov/pmc/articles/PMC4492928/.

The best way to reinforce new learnings and have a tangible impact from new knowledge and skills is to apply theory to practice. But that is simpler said than done. The biggest reason why people are not trying new things at work is not because they don't want to. It's because they are not allowed to or not feel motivated to do so.

Following a simple framework of learn, practice, and do, it's up to leaders to create the right culture that doesn't only enable learning but also enables practicing and making it part of the default ways of working:

- **Learn:** Providing different formats and channels for learning. Ask for feedback on what content and formats are the preferred options.

- **Practice:** Provide opportunities to practice what has been learned in theory in a safe space. Team meetings and peer-to-peer coaching are great opportunities to do so.

- **Do:** Make learning and applying new things part of the job descriptions and measure performance based on innovative applications of new skills and knowledge.

For example, a data scientist learns about a new algorithm and commits to getting upskilled in the theory and application of that algorithm. She presents her new knowledge in a team meeting, and her colleagues and manager encourage her newly acquired knowledge in a project where it's suited. Through continuous peer-to-peer coaching with a colleague, she gains the confidence to apply it and her successful application is reflected in her performance evaluation as part of her upskilling efforts.

We must do more than wait for our employees and coworkers to take the initiative to learn, practice, and do. We must also create an environment conducive to and encouraging such behavior. In addition to catering to various learning styles, it's crucial to create a "safe space" where students can practice in an environment that supports them, such as through team meetings and peer-to-peer coaching. Lastly, we should make it the default by including innovation based on applying new knowledge in job descriptions and performance evaluations. We can achieve a continual incentive for progress by enabling proactive learning activities and enforcing them through job descriptions.

All these decisions should be captured as "guiding principles" as part of the data strategy—a document that encourages certain mindsets and behaviors and considers statements regarding priorities and expectations toward all contributors and team members.

An academy concept as a way to bring it together

A way to upskill in terms of data literacy and business acumen and to encourage learning, practicing, and doing all at once is by establishing an "academy" concept in an organization.

The idea behind the academy concept is simple and consists of four main aspects: modularized learning, group environments, incentives through gamification, and communities of practice. Let me elaborate:

- **Modularized learning:** Breaking down topics into smaller, shorter modules removes the fear of commitment and increases the frequency of rewards after finishing each module. These modules should each fulfill a purpose on both theoretical and practical levels, and the outcome of each should enable students to apply what they learned. For example, instead of doing a one-year-long course on "How to become a Data Analyst," it can be 12 four-week courses that each have a focus on hard and soft skills, such as "Basic analysis functions in Excel" or "Applying SQL to Financial Databases."

- **Group environments:** Whether the modules are live classes or on-demand courses, establish a group setting and encourage and facilitate peer-to-peer exchanges. The benefit of learning with a group is that it can increase motivation to learn by sharing the experience, and students can hold each other accountable for each other's progress, so the likelihood that students drop out of their learning activity is lower. For example, establish group assignments for specific modules that encourage everyone to bring their existing practical experience into group exchanges.

- **Incentives through gamification:** Besides the practical aspect of having learned new skills and knowledge, people love to express their intellectual progress and achievements. Establishing a structured approach to badges, certificates, and special acknowledgments can do that. For example, every student receives a badge after finishing a module and then gets a signed certificate by senior leaders after finishing a series of defined modules with a common topic. Those who are especially fast and disciplined in their learning efforts receive special acknowledgment in the next company town hall or team meeting.

- **Communities of practice:** The learning and group interactions should not stop after learning specific modules, so creating "alumni networks" as communities of practice can extend the knowledge exchange and prevent siloed ways of working in the organization. Positioning these exchanges and communities as a benefit for growth and not just for business impact can motivate students intrinsically to participate. For example, a monthly meet-up and chat group of all current and aspiring data analysts to exchange best practices and innovations and help each other with challenges.

The question that may be on your mind now is, "Who is sponsoring all of that?" That's a good question, and the short answer is that discussing how to pay for staff training and development should be a major element of any data strategy's overall financing discussions.

Another crucial factor is not starting an academy as a massive undertaking right away. In addition to being more cost-effective at the outset, piloting with a single module and one learning group can become a proof of concept to boost trust in the program and provide valuable insight into how to make the academy concept a reality.

Equipping people with the right knowledge and skills should make them more proactive innovators and reduce resistance to change management efforts. In conclusion, including an academy concept as part of a data strategy should be positioned as a necessary investment, with the return on investment being an increased speed in innovation and change adoption.

Leadership skills ≠ Subject matter expertise

My music teacher in elementary school once took the class to visit the local orchestra. We were all asked to stand next to our favorite instrument to make the exercise more fun. The children started lining up behind the violinists, the trumpetists, and other musicians, and I decided to stand behind the conductor. I thought the conductor stick was the most fascinating instrument –a stick that could control the other instruments through swinging movements! The conductor himself was very amused. He handed me the conductor stick and continued guiding my hands to conduct the orchestra. I had a lot of fun, but I also learned an important lesson: leading is very different than actually doing it yourself.

We reward people who are good at doing their jobs with promotions into roles with people and leadership responsibilities. Often, we recognize too late (or never) that being an expert in something doesn't necessarily mean you know how to lead others.

While there are different ways to teach and coach leadership skills, what's more important is that these skills are part of evaluating people's readiness to get promoted into leadership roles. Evaluation should not only happen from their direct managers but instead be based as much as possible on a holistic review from their peers, collaborators, stakeholders, and, if they exist, their current subordinates.

Too often, we hear horror stories about data leaders who micromanage, are too aggressive or not assertive enough in setting directions, or do not protect or overprotect their team members in times of conflict. It's not completely their fault, though, because I believe that they're all doing what they think is right—they are just missing references to best practices in data leadership.

In the context of a people-empowering data strategy, we need servant leaders who can balance the strategic context of driving value with data with empowering and enabling experts to fulfill their potential by proactively contributing to data efforts. The right leadership behavior, and in relation to that feedback behavior, should also be captured in the "guiding principles" of the data strategy.

Confidence as friend or foe of competence

Once we make progress in a certain area of expertise, our competence is enhanced and ready to be converted into action. Another important aspect of doing that successfully is confidence—confidence in one's skills and in making the right decisions and actions.

There are two effects related to confidence and competence to consider as risks:

- Dunning-Kruger-Effect[4] describes overconfidence in relation to someone's competence

- Imposter-Syndrome[5] describes the under-confidence in relation to someone's competence

Put into a qualitative graph of competence versus confidence, it's evident that there is a "balanced" line where knowledge and confidence are proportionally growing, and deviating off towards higher or lower confidence constitutes these two effects:

---

[4] Kruger, Justin & Dunning, David. (2000). Unskilled and Unaware of It: How Difficulties in Recognizing One's Own Incompetence Lead to Inflated Self-Assessments. Journal of Personality and Social Psychology. 77. 1121-34. 10.1037//0022-3514.77.6.1121.

[5] https://www.ncbi.nlm.nih.gov/pmc/articles/PMC10236681/.

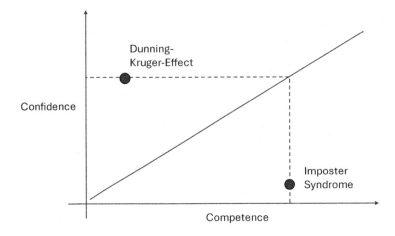

From a data strategy point of view, these two effects can have dire consequences. People acting and deciding based on overconfidence can lead to a lack of information considered and not including the opinions of experts, leading to bad choices regarding data. When people are underconfident, they fear deciding and acting because they don't feel competent enough, so we never fully utilize people's expertise to take the best actions regarding data possible, or decisions are taken too slowly and too late.

More importantly, these two effects are deeply rooted in people's past experiences and personalities, so it is rare for someone to reflect on and recognize them independently.

The solution to this challenge is to create the right environment for honest and constructive feedback. Acknowledging each other's achievements and providing honest feedback and guidance when someone's confidence is either abundant or insufficient is yet another great opportunity to leverage "guiding principles" to encourage and reward the right behavior and consideration of feedback.

The different "hats" to wear when working in data

There are many well-defined data job titles, for example, "data analyst," "data engineer," and "data scientist." All these job titles come with a list of "hard skills," such as specific coding languages and conceptual understanding, and often now also with a list of "soft skills," such as communication skills or stakeholder management skills. These describe a list of "requirements" for people who want to take on these roles well, but they don't describe what applying those skills looks like.

This is where I think the description of different "hats to wear" in a data role helps describe situations and objectives in which the previously mentioned skills are applied. Differentiating between different "hats" also helps prepare and specify collaborator interactions.

The more these hats can be defined based on experience with different situations, objectives, and skills needed, the more data professionals can be prepared upfront for successful interactions. Framing skills through the lens of practical application in the day-to-day doesn't only let people grow faster through practical experience. It also makes day-to-day tasks more effective and, hopefully, has an actual business impact.

From a data strategy point of view, these "hats" not only help to identify which skills and experiences are needed for specific job descriptions and hiring decisions, but they also help to navigate upskilling and coaching opportunities for

all team members when they're required to act in a certain
way but don't know how yet.

"Hat to wear"	Situation (examples)	Objective (examples)	Skills to apply (examples)
Therapist	Requirements clarification	Understanding and quantifying the pain points of stakeholders	Empathy, Active listening, Interviewing, Data communication
Project Manager	Scoping and execution of the project	Ensuring project success	Project management, stakeholder management
Negotiator	Agreeing on collaboration	Define operating model	Empathy, conflict management
Detective	Investigation of data problems	Identify root causes and define sustainable solutions	Critical thinking, structured working, SQL, Python
Communicator	Townhall presentation	Getting wider stakeholder buy-in	Presentation, public speaking, data visualization
Developer	Writing a SQL query	Define technical business rules	SQL, Tool navigation, DataOps
Mediator	Navigating conflict between different data parties	Reach agreement for policy	Conflict management, empathy, active listening

Career paths and job rotations

Once people are upskilled and have practiced their new skills, they are ready to change jobs–either changing to a different area or getting promoted to different roles, but too often are people only recognized for their practical experience in their respective current jobs, not for the new skills they acquired to apply in different contexts.

One reason for that is the bias towards "the other side"–and by that, I mean that business people and data people see each other as very far away when, in reality, all data objectives in today's world are building bridges stronger than ever before. And let's face it, if we would bring more business expertise into data teams, and more data expertise into business teams, we would immediately see a positive impact–I have experienced this myself a few times.

Another reason for the difficulty of having the "business" and "data" worlds exchange talents more is the individual motivation and objectives of hiring managers. Too often, managers are still intimidated by people with more expertise in certain areas, and they are too critical of the job candidate's knowledge and skills because they like to compare to their own state of knowledge. Setting up standardized, more inclusive job assessment criteria with actual cross-functional panels to assess candidates can help neutralize that bias.

The final reason is that the overall talent and people strategy does not support lateral function-switching career moves and focuses strongly on same-department or same-function career paths. A "special hiring culture" for data will not work if the rest of the company hires in very conservative and rigid ways. Essentially, there needs to be a strategy that supports talent exchanges in different degrees–from job shadowing to short-term assignments to actual talent transitions to other departments.

Enabling the right career and growth paths is important because if employees can't grow, they will leave at some point. In many cases, that means losing the ambitious and versatile ones in your workforce. Removing bias and believing in cross-functional talent exchanges must also become part of the "people" part of the data strategy.

Human resources as a key collaborator

All the aspects mentioned in this "Competence" chapter have one thing in common: they are usually decided upon by the Human Resources (HR) team. The main potential for improvement I see across many current organizations is to see the HR team not only as a hiring and escalation function—they can also be really valuable enablers. Many of the aspects related to learning, leadership, academy concepts, coaching, or mentoring are part of the programs that HR and people teams are responsible for anyway. Leveraging the existing mandate and expertise from these colleagues can be an effective way to reach your competence-related goal. It also has the added benefit of showcasing cross-functional collaboration to make data valuable. More on collaboration in the next chapter.

Three

Collaboration

The previous chapter was about empowering specific individuals and their competence and confidence. This chapter is about interpersonal relationships and interactions. Collaboration, that is.

Collaboration is more important than ever in data because despite how the data team was seen as responsible for everything related to data in the past, we realize that data is everyone's responsibility and that people who don't have "data" in their title might have much more impact and influence on data than those that have official "data roles."

Since the dawn of humankind, working together has been ingrained in human behavior and culture. It's only through artificially defined power dynamics and conflicting motivations that we see collaboration not working in organizations, including data endeavors. It's time that we don't try to offset the intrinsic need for collaboration but instead leverage it to unleash the power of true collaboration.

Let's dive into some practical advice around data collaboration.

Embedding data collaboration into the talent lifecycle

Collaboration skills, especially around data, are something that people are born with, but many still need additional guidance on how to apply them in a specific business context. When it comes to data, teaching and guiding people to collaborate in the right way can never start too early.

This is why periodically doing collaboration coaching is not enough. Instead, we should focus on the overall talent lifecycle to continuously embed data collaboration advice and impulses.

On a high level, the talent lifecycle consists of three main stages: talent acquisition, onboarding, and performance management. We do different activities at each stage to ensure individuals are collaborating correctly.

As the great organizational psychologist Simon Sinek once said, "Hire for attitude, train for skills." This also applies to data, where it's much harder to change someone's mindset and attitude than training someone with specific hard skills in terms of coding or tool usage. We should assess data collaboration for empathy, teamwork, and conflict resolution skills during the job interview stage. This could happen, for example, by asking the candidate to discuss a conflict they solved or performing a role play to see how well the candidate collaborates.

During onboarding of new joiners, it's equally important to indirectly and directly establish data collaboration as a default way of working. That means, for example, including data teams prominently when main functions are introduced and using facts and numbers from data projects by non-data teams. The new joiners should feel that data is taken seriously in this organization, and they will act accordingly from the get-go.

Lastly, the performance of employees can and should also be measured based on their collaboration around data. This can happen by sharing objectives between data teams and business teams that are cascaded down to individual levels, thereby encouraging and enforcing a collaboration that leads to success for which collaborators can share the credit. Additionally, sharing best practices and experiences around data collaboration should be encouraged to allow everyone to apply what worked before to reach their collaboration goals.

Understanding data collaboration by every contributing individual is crucial for any data strategy. Assessing the level of understanding and adopted mindset and behavior regarding data collaboration is an important step to defining realistic goals– and, most importantly, it helps you identify fundamental risks for the success of your data strategy.

The easiest way isn't always the "right" way

In many ways, human beings are like water. We naturally follow the path of least resistance to get things done, even when we know it's not the "right" way. I once burned myself with boiling water while cooking pasta in a small pan just because I was too lazy to get the bigger dirty pot out of the dishwasher and wash it by hand.

It's not too different when it comes to data collaboration. Doing things easy and fast without considering the consequences is often preferred over doing it the "right" way—which usually also means the more valuable way. We shouldn't blame the people who choose the easy way because the benefits and motivation for doing it the "right" way are often unclear.

We could blame it on the discrepancy between short-term and long-term thinking, but even then, the question is, "Why should I care about the long term if I am only impacted by the short term?"

For example, If someone wants to distribute a dataset they're currently working on with their colleagues, the "easiest" way is to export the data into an Excel® or CSV file and then share it via e-mail. The dangers of this approach are that there are no security or access control mechanisms on this data anymore and that many new versions of the facts now exist. We can avoid that if there is a governed and managed table that everybody can access and share access to it or create a more tailored view for a specific use case.

No matter how much we want to enforce the right behavior, when it comes to data, people will always find a way to go around the enforcement mechanisms. So, the only way to make the right behavior last is through intrinsic motivation. This requires a clear understanding of the benefits and implications of dealing with data in the "right way."

The "right way" is often captured in policies, guidelines, and checklists. These documents can be very detailed and include clear instructions on how to do things, but often they do not include the "why" or more information about "What's in it for me?" If we, for example, create a policy around data privacy, besides information around the sensitivity of personal information and the mandatory application of anonymization, obfuscating, and masking mechanisms, there should be a section around the benefit of dealing with personal data correctly. We can address the regulatory, brand reputation, and ethical angles in this case.

What does that mean for collaboration? Doing things the "right" way usually involves more than one system or team, which requires cross-functional collaboration. And if that collaboration is unpleasant, such as having to interact with ticket systems without a clue when your ticket will be worked on, or getting calendar invites rejected by the collaboration team all the time without any explanation, then I might as well not do it the right way anymore.

There are many ways to make collaboration easier. For example:

- List the responsible teams and respective contact details in the policies and maintain that information as well. Knowing there is someone to talk to can be helpful.

- Don't hide completely behind ticketing systems for business-critical processes. Instead, use it for managing workload and priorities, but continue using human interactions to address human nuances needed, such as translations, specifications, or clarifications.

- Balance service versus self-service consciously because experts should always do some things with the right experience, while other less critical and tedious tasks could be either automated or done by the requester themselves. It's a trade-off between a greater workload for the person trying to "do it right" versus a longer time to achieve it due to the servicing team becoming a bottleneck for too many requests.

So if we want to encourage everyone to do the "right" things, it should not only be clear what the benefit is, but we should also make it easy to do the "right" thing by establishing operating models and ways of working around it—and make it official and mandatory in a data strategy.

Doing the "right" thing for data

"Right" is data quality when it comes to data. Let me elaborate.

Data quality is the degree to which data is "fit for purpose." It sounds like a straightforward definition, but the human aspect is immensely important for this concept. Not only does the "purpose" have to be known, which means there has to be full transparency across all use cases and the respective requirements towards the data–the "fit" can only be measured and monitored once everybody agrees on what "fit" actually means. Data quality comes down to human actions that lead to transparency and human agreement.

There is no truly objective "right" thing to do. Only through data collaboration does everybody agree on the "right" things, so subjectivity turns into objectivity.

Documentation of these agreements and what leads to the decision can help others understand what is right and what is wrong and save precious time and effort by following the right path from the beginning. This is why policies should not only be another useless, too-detailed document that everybody is forced to read but should also be communicated to ensure success in all projects and initiatives. Compliance with these policies should be communicated as achievements.

If we are calling out doing the "wrong" thing as uncompliant behavior, then it's only fair that we acknowledge doing the "right" thing as good behavior or even as best practices for any related future projects.

One way to enforce the "right" things without disrupting business as usual is to leverage automation, often called "policy as code." The challenge with that concept is that policies are usually in prose written documents, and turning them into code would imply that machines can easily read and derive rules and mechanisms from them. This is not possible, at least not yet.

Making policy automation happen today requires two additional layers: translating policies into code through interim states, such as rule-based language and machine-readable text, and ownership for reviewing, maintaining, and updating all the policy codes and their applications. Both layers require a very specific set of skills (to quote the great Liam Neeson in "Taken"), and even with the right talent to take over these responsibilities, I think the best way would be to have both the human motivation based approach as well as the policy-as-code automatically enforced approach.

Policies are never a sexy topic, but they are great levers of success for a data strategy due to their enforcing nature, further solidified by senior leadership sign-offs. They should not be seen only as authoritative measures but as vehicles for cascading down decisions and behaviors for every data strategy contributor.

Service or Self-Service?

Data collaboration can take many forms, but one aspect seems to always be top of mind for anyone working in data strategy: Should data capabilities be treated as a service that a data team fulfills for their business stakeholders, or should they be treated as self-service, where the business teams get their own data capabilities to create value from data more autonomously?

Balancing between one service team versus multiple empowered self-service teams leads to the underlying question: *Centralization* or *Decentralization*? To be more specific, the question is to what degree data capabilities and responsibilities are centralized and to what degree those are decentralized.

Because a decision about the organizational structure directly impacts the team's belonging, it immediately impacts where the expertise lies—and it naturally implies a dynamic relationship between the data experts and the business stakeholders. In other words, the organizational structure decides if data becomes a service or self-service.

Both the concepts of "data as a service" and "enabled data self-service" started as ideologies with positive intentions until reality showed its negative consequences.

When a central data team exists as the center of all data expertise, all business stakeholders can request whatever they need from this rockstar expert team. But when businesses become more data-driven, the hunger for data-derived insights increases, and the central data team becomes a bottleneck. Hiring new people could never keep up with the increase in data requests, and everybody knew it wasn't scalable.

So we went in the opposite direction: the solution has to be decentralization. Let the business teams do their own data tasks and projects. First, business stakeholders realized they didn't have the necessary skills or talents to do it, so they all got their own data experts in their teams. For data professionals, it felt refreshing to be among business experts and the only "geek" among them. These data experts started understanding the needs of their immediate business colleagues. They realized how they would collect data needed to be as unique as their departments. New data infrastructures, databases, and analytical applications sprang up like mushrooms with one important problem—none of those were particularly useful for others, and most importantly, they didn't work well with each other.

So, the world finally understood the need for a balance between centralization and decentralization, and we ended up with concepts like *Data Mesh* and *Data Fabric* that try to incorporate the best of both worlds. Thought leaders and businesses love talking about these two because everybody wants to avoid making the same mistakes as in the past.

But I don't want to dissect and evaluate centralization and decentralization concepts too in-depth—this book is about the "human side" of data. So, let's talk about a mindset shift that organizations and corporations should adopt to avoid repeatedly falling into the same traps. For me, there is one middle ground between "service" and "self-service," which is **co-creation**.

What has always bothered me about the term *service* is the transactional nature of the concept itself. You ask me to do something and I do it. You give me an arbitrary amount that we both agree my effort is worth and then this transaction is finished. I serviced, and you got serviced–it's done. This might be necessary as a concept between sellers and buyers (and it's a foundational pillar of today's economics). Still, we should move away from transactional collaboration to trust-based co-creational collaboration when it comes to internal collaboration.

Co-creation implies two things: that something truly new is created (otherwise, it's just a "rehashing" of something existing), and that there's an equal standing between the co-creation parties. Whether data skills are centralized or decentralized, when business expertise and data expertise come together, there should always be an agreement and commitment to co-create solutions. A verbal (or even formal) contract about co-creation also has the benefit that it can survive any restructuring because it works within or across departments.

For example, a marketing manager asks a data analyst to create insights and recommendations for her upcoming campaign. In a centralized setup, the data analyst would accept the request but would need to prioritize it against other requests. The data analyst would also potentially struggle with the business context since marketing is just one of the use cases the person is working on. In a decentralized set-up, the data analyst would create a table or dashboard for the marketing manager to create the insights and recommendations on their own, which the marketing manager may or may not be capable of, and lower confidence in analyzing data could lead to challenges.

If there is a co-creational relationship about this, it would imply that both parties are committed and accountable for the success. Regardless of whether it is centralized or decentralized, both sides would complement each other with their skills and knowledge, and the collaboration would be rooted in a common goal, not individual goals.

I don't think there is one golden solution to balance centralization and decentralization of data responsibilities. The chances are that for a given organization, this will continuously change anyway, depending on the data maturity, the culture, and the industry. We can change the mindset of collaboration and move away from transactional services to co-creational collaboration—another strong "guiding principle" for a data strategy.

Roles in the circle of (data) life

The Circle of Life is not only one of my favorite songs from one of my favorite Disney movies ("Lion King" fans rejoice!), but it also has a special meaning when it comes to data.

The data lifecycle can encompass many systems, processes, and, most importantly, many people. Because data usually replicates when flowing, it can quickly happen that data flows everywhere, and nobody has an overview of where all the data is.

That lack of transparency can have serious consequences, not only from a regulation and risk point of view by not being aware of illegal and uncompliant actions being taken with the data, but also from an efficiency point of view when redundant data sets appear everywhere, costing unnecessary efforts and storage space over and over again.

We spot this by defining clear responsibilities. People might not even know they have such a critical role in the data lifecycle. In simple terms, there are three main roles in the data lifecycle of any data type:

- **Data Producer:** somebody creates data records for the first time to bring them into an organization's data ecosystem (for example, a sales representative creating a new customer record).

- **Data Processor:** somebody transforms or reshapes existing data for a different technical application (for example, a data engineer building a pipeline that transforms customer data from the CRM system into the data lake).

- **Data Consumer:** somebody uses the data to take actions or make better decisions to drive direct value for the organization (for example, a sales manager changing the pricing strategy of products based on sales data).

These roles are not mutually exclusive, so someone producing data might afterward process it and consume it for their own purposes. Having these different roles means there should be a clear guideline on what they should or should not do.

Data producers need to be accountable for their input—they are responsible for creating correct data records that cascade down to systems and data consumers around the company. Knowing certain data points are more critical than others, data producers need to diligently prioritize the accuracy and reliability of the data they create, and they need to responsibly correct the records if any concern from a data consumption point of view is triggered.

Data processors need to consider how the data producers created the data in the first place while transforming it so as not to break the integrity of the original creation. They need to be diligent in documenting and communicating the data transformation and leave contextual information for any downstream system and users when interpreting the data's usage.

Data consumers should not assume anything about the data and should be aware of any contextual information left by data producers and data processors. They have the important role of providing feedback if any changes are required to the data. Data consumers are responsible for being clear about their data requirements and maintaining and owning those requirements.

When we think of data, we often think of analytics and AI. Still, it's important to understand that data also has a very operational purpose to support critical business processes, often involving people who do not bring data expertise. The roles can be very different across the analytical and operational side of data.

Examples for data lifecycle roles	Analytical	Operational
Data producer	Sales representative creates customer data	Sales representative creates customer data
Data processor	Data engineer connects CRM system to Data Lake	Software developer connects CRM to Marketing Platform
Data consumer	Data scientist creates customer segmentation	Marketing manager sends out emails to specific customers

Because the use cases for the same type of data can be very different, the requirements can be conflicting towards the data as well–and the only prevention is to create transparency of these requirements and to agree on a solution that respects all requirements. If not, one thing could lead to another, and to meet the requirements of a new use case, you change the data so it destroys a critical business process that can be very costly.

I discussed data literacy in a previous chapter. Fulfilling the responsibilities in any data lifecycle role is one of the most important reasons to develop and apply data literacy.

From a data strategy point of view, there should be some dedicated human facilitation to bring all sides of the data lifecycle together and not only let systems talk to each other but also make the human beings the side characters. Horizontal teams like data strategy teams, data governance teams, and data culture teams can all bring data stakeholders together.

We know that the importance, size, and number of use cases around data will drastically increase in the next years, so dedicating some efforts to building and maintaining the human connection around data along the lifecycle is a good option.

"Follow the pain" as an impact-driven approach

One of the best ways to build the right collaboration culture around data is to solve problems. Sounds simple, right? In reality, data teams are often too excited about building solutions that forget about the problems to solve. This leads to advanced and cutting-edge projects from the data teams, while business teams still struggle with basic data problems requiring manual efforts to maintain simple core business processes.

So, to have a connection to business value through working with the business teams and nurturing a collaborative spirit, a data strategy should guide and evangelize mindset and process to solve problems.

The first step to solving problems is to identify them. Hence, I call "follow the pain" a general mindset and philosophy that makes data valuable and collaborative.

It's all based on the assumption that in any organization, there is someone who is really frustrated about a data problem. Data teams should find that person and work with them. Great collaboration will happen because of two reasons: 1) the frustration of the impacted person is so high that they would do anything to get their problem out of the way, including working with the data team, and 2) they've been dealing with the problem for so long that they have very clear requirements about what the solution of the problem should achieve, and what the impact of the problem is–and thereby the value of the solution.

Once a solution is co-created, this person will be so happy that good word of mouth about the data team is guaranteed. That advocacy ideally will lead to more business teams hearing about the great work of the data teams, and over time, more "pain points" appear–then you build a backlog and a roadmap for steady success and achievements.

By applying the "following the pain" approach, collaboration will improve, and a new default engagement model with stakeholders will surface that emphasizes active listening to problems and empathy for business challenges. Issue diagnosis and remediation approaches should be formally defined in the data strategy and used as a reference for any related type of data collaboration.

"Three musketeers" of data issue root causes

All data issues in the world can be traced back to three root causes: human error, process error, or technical error. These causes are not mutually exclusive. For example, one problem could be due to all three root causes.

The reasons for differentiating between the root causes is that the solutions for them look very differently:

- **Human error**–characterized by an error made through direct manipulation of data by a human hand. For example, when a product manager creates a product record with a typo in the product name. The solution often includes training and guidelines to encourage more diligent behavior. Technology can be applied to guard rail manual data entry a bit more.

- **Process error**–characterized by a structural misalignment between the actual and required process. For example, only update data weekly when daily updated data is needed. The solution often includes a harmonization of processes rooted in transparency and alignment.

- **Technical error**–characterized by an error caused by an automated workflow. For example, when a data pipeline breaks down, data is not being updated at all. The solution often includes some actual technical development and implementing a monitoring solution to identify and tackle root causes more timely and proactively.

Although only "human error" has the word "human" in its name, all three root cause types connect with human skills: critical thinking to investigate the root causes and human agreement to decide on a solution to fix the root cause problems.

The best way to move from reactively mitigating these issues to preventing these issues proactively is by identifying patterns across the different data issue root cause types, and defining process blueprints on how to get from investigation to solutions—by applying what makes us human beings special: critical thinking.

Finding your "data purpose" to make strategic choices

There are increasingly more advanced and exciting things that you can do with data. Still, just because it's exciting to do, it's not necessarily the RIGHT thing to do, especially in an organizational context.

To have a more collaborative approach towards making strategic choices towards data while balancing between opportunities and risks, I created a framework for finding "your data purpose." It's inspired by the famous Japanese philosophy of "Ikigai,"[6] but adapted to the context of data.

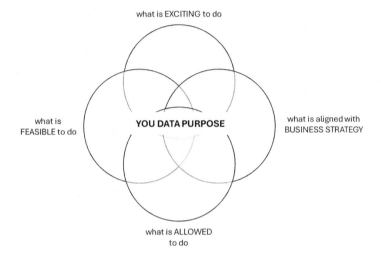

The "data purpose" postulates that any strategic choice about data should consider four aspects before moving forward:

- What is *EXCITING* to do: Everyone in an organization has ideas about what to do with data, and it's all based on the very pure emotion of excitement. Newer, cutting-edge, state-of-the-art data stuff is exciting–and it should be acknowledged and captured. This aspect is usually driven by data, AI experts, and senior leaders who are easily hyped about the newest technologies.

---

[6] García, H., Miralles, F. (2017). Ikigai: The Japanese Secret to a Long and Happy Life. United Kingdom: Random House.

- What is *ALIGNED WITH BUSINESS STRATEGY*: Not all the exciting things to do will support the organization's goals. This is the first "filter" to ensure that data efforts align with business objectives while keeping the excitement from the previous aspect. C-level leaders, business unit leaders, and corporate governance teams usually drive this aspect.

- What is *ALLOWED TO DO*: There are many internal and external constraints on what should and should not be done with data, for good reasons. Regulations and policies are the only way to prevent risky actions from leading to issues that society cannot recover from. Legal teams, information security teams, and any roles with ethical and DEI responsibilities usually drive this aspect.

- What is *FEASIBLE TO DO*: You can achieve any good data objective if an organization's technology and data management maturity enable it. This requires honest reflection and assessment of realistic goals to set given the current state, even with the best intentions to grow and mature. This aspect is usually driven by IT, data governance, enterprise architecture, and other roles that regularly assess technology stacks and capability maturities.

What does that look like in action? Here are some examples:

- An AI-powered customer profiling for credit scoring might be exciting to do, aligns with business strategy, and is feasible—but ethically, there might be a negative bias towards certain demographics of people, so it should be considered "not allowed to do"

- A real-time business intelligence dashboard for live eCommerce pricing decisions on Black Friday might meet all criteria, but it is not "feasible to do" due to the missing components of data quality and integrity monitoring that would ensure the data is trustworthy

- A monthly exported Excel file about how the daily temperatures were in a region from the past 30 days might be feasible and allowed to do, but it probably doesn't align with business objectives and is definitely not exciting

Not only can goals be set in a more realistic and achievable manner by considering these four aspects while making strategic choices about data, but this approach also enforces a collaboration with key stakeholders of the data team already during the planning phase, and not just in the implementation phase when it's usually also including some sunk costs and requires a lot more efforts to manage newly identified risks rather than to have considered them in the first place.

Finding purpose is a very human thing, so why shouldn't we apply it to data as well? Capturing this purpose in a data strategy makes it official and can bring everyone on board to collaborate in the same direction.

Think big, but start small

Once strategic choices about data have been made collaboratively, everyone is happy with agreeing on common objectives for data, and the natural instinct often pushes us just to get started on all of them at the same time. The result is often that many things are getting started, but none of them make progress fast enough or never get finished. This not only undermines the data strategy's importance but also hurts the data teams' credibility in what to achieve. To prevent this situation, we must define how to get started and in what sequence to conduct activities to make the data strategy a reality. We need to avoid "boiling the ocean" and instead tackle data initiatives one "bucket" at a time.

Planning a proper roadmap is important not only to structure the work and synchronize the priorities for all data team members but also to be transparent with all data stakeholders and manage their expectations.

So, how can you decide in what order to roll out the data initiatives and projects to make your data strategy a reality? The key lies in considering three aspects: complexity, impact, and dependencies. Every data initiative and project needs to be evaluated not only in the efforts needed to be successful and the impact the project has—it needs to be clear also if a given project depends on the success of another project, or if this given project is a prerequisite for other projects.

When data projects are evaluated based on these three aspects, it is important to consider not only the technical aspects but also the "human" aspect. For example:

- From a human point of view, complexity could mean missing skillsets and lack of required talents, uncollaborative working cultures in different teams, or misaligning common goals across teams.

- From a human point of view, the impact could mean a personal reward, a contribution to societal good, or an increase in productivity for specific teams.

- Dependencies from a human point of view could mean undefined roles and responsibilities, lack of previous collaboration experience between co-creational teams, or high manual effort needed because of a missing technology.

To create a roadmap to implement a data strategy, the key is to find a balance between achieving continuous achievements through low-complexity, high-impact, and low-dependency projects and tackling the higher-complexity, lower-impact, and higher-dependency ones more carefully, taking into account longer implementation times.

"Ad-hoc requests" and demand management

Okay, now you have a plan. But in the fast and ever-changing world of data, additional things always pop up that require timely actions not anticipated before. This is why a data strategy roadmap needs a balance between planned initiatives and ad-hoc requests.

Operational teams, such as Global Business Services, DevOps, or DataOps are all used to having a certain demand management process to manage requests, often involving a ticketing system. These systems are a great way to keep an overview and prioritization of different requests. Still, the natural tendency is to reduce human contact and to treat these tickets as to-do lists rather than opportunities for one human being to help another through interaction.

While visiting my relatives in China in the fall of 2023, I was astounded by the degree to which everything was digitalized—all payments were digital, smart screens were everywhere, and phone charging stations were everywhere you looked. So I went into a coffee shop to order a cappuccino with the Barista, but he pointed to a QR code on the wall and said: "Only orders via app. I don't have time to talk to our customers. I have to deliver a certain frequency of orders per hour, sorry." After I ordered digitally and got my delicious coffee quickly, I couldn't help but feel like I ended up in a dystopian future.

Data solutions, in contrast to coffee, are rarely a one-size-fits-all approach. Without human interaction to discuss and agree on a solution and to show appreciation for each other, a solution to a problem might have been implemented. Still, it might not have been the best or the most sustainable solution.

The key lies in the incentive and measure of success of demand management. Often, a KPI for operational teams is the number of tickets processed and resolved in a given time period, but measuring that alone puts too much emphasis on efficiency and not enough on effectiveness. A way to balance that is to add metrics for success measurement based on human feedback, such as a satisfaction score based on a survey for each ticket. Lastly, human interactions should not be avoided, but people should be encouraged to be able to regularly grasp the human nuances of data requests as well as understand important contexts between the lines.

To tie this back to the previous chapter, the planned roadmap activities and newly processed and solved ad-hoc requests should not exist in silos but should inform each other. The planned roadmap activities might provide new capabilities and information that can act as a solution for many ad-hoc requests, and the requirements from different ad-hoc requests might inform the development of new skill sets and capabilities in the data strategy roadmap.

Success is a matter of mindset

Having the feeling of achievement and progress is a key aspect of motivation. Having made significant progress and an important step towards the strategic data objectives should not be taken lightly as a task done on a to-do list, but should be celebrated by acknowledging individual contributors and recognizing the power of cross-functional collaboration through shared credit. Addressing these milestones should also signal to the rest of the organization how effective and important data collaboration is.

Let's only look at strategic milestones in our data strategy, such as project milestones, data management maturity, or a data quality monitoring solution. Months can pass waiting between milestones, often putting the patience and motivation of data team members to the test. Impatience and lack of motivation can have serious consequences. People who lose their drive and passion for their day-to-day tasks can easily be less diligent and less collaborative, leading to a serious risk for the success of a data strategy.

The key to preventing this is by defining more broadly and inclusively what success means. Besides the big important strategic milestones, smaller steps towards those and other more human factors can and should be successes, such as having given training with other departments, having increased efficiency incrementally, getting official commitment from collaborators, or having generated new ideas. If we recognize these smaller steps as progress, we also include them when we talk about our progress and achievements, and the rest of the organization recognizes progress and achievements more continuously, creating advocacy for the data efforts.

The power of communities

Organizational structures help structure responsibilities, accountabilities, and processes, but they constantly change due to frequent restructurings. Just when everyone got used to a new daily routine and an established set of key collaborators, the next "reorg" could throw it all over, and you would need to adapt again. Human beings are animals of habit, and change is hard.

To counteract the uncertainty of a continuously changing organization, it helps to build an organization-agnostic layer (community) of collaboration to gather people with similar interests, job titles, or challenges.

This is not a new concept, especially in tech organizations where "communities of practice" have been proven to increase idea creation, lead to increased quality of knowledge and advice, more problem-solving, and create a common context[7].

From an organizational point of view, communities of practice are great for knowledge sharing and best practice adoption, making data efforts more effective and efficient. However, from a human needs point of view, communities are great for two other reasons: curing loneliness and the reward of helping each other.

---

[7] Millen, David & Fontaine, Michael & Muller, Michael. (2002). Understanding the benefit and costs of communities of practice. Commun. ACM. 45. 69-73. 10.1145/505248.505276.

Many data roles in today's job landscape are not working in one team (anymore). Where roles like data engineers and data scientists were in the past in one central function and were able to "nerd out" together, the new landscape of going for decentralized empowered data domains means that these roles are now distributed within business teams. Other roles like data owners or data stewards have always been in the business functions, and they've been bravely on the "data hat" in an environment where no one else could or wants to do it.

In either case, being the "odd one out" can feel lonely. And that loneliness is further emphasized when things are not going well, and some help is needed. Who can you ask for help if you're the only expert on the team? Instead of asking for favors and building up a support network, which not everyone is eager to do or good at, a community can become a natural place not to feel alone anymore and to naturally ask for help among people who like to help.

Examples in practice are data steward communities, data owner networks, or data engineer communities of practice–what made them all successful is to make clear to everyone that it's rooted in humanity and that it's supposed to connect people and provide each other with help. Similar to learning and upskilling, the investment of time and energy into communities should be encouraged and sponsored by the leadership–otherwise, it will always clash with "more important things."

Organizational structures always change, but communities should be more stable–and they should be acknowledged in a data strategy as a defined and valuable part of a hierarchy-agnostic operating model.

Data culture needs to be role modeled

A data culture is the "collective behaviors and beliefs of people within an organization who value, practice, and encourage the use of data to improve decision-making."[8] For me, a good data culture has always been both a driver and an outcome of a good data strategy. In the context of the 5Cs framework, a good data culture relates to all aspects, yet mostly collaboration.

There are many great books, articles, and thought leaders on creating a good data culture, but all opinions and approaches have one thing in common: they will not improve or progress without the influence of senior leadership because culture always needs to be driven top-down.

And it requires more than just nice words from the CEO about how data-driven the company is. It also requires active role-modeling and guiding others to take decision-making with and about data seriously. I like to encourage senior leaders to adopt a simple "Talk-Act-Guide" framework when it comes to data, which means:

- **Talking** explicitly about the importance of data and fact-based decisions that involve data implicitly.

---

[8] ISLAM, D. S. (2024). Data Culture: Develop an Effective Data-Driven Organization. United Kingdom: Kogan Page.

- **Acting** as a role model by demonstrating not only making decisions by collaborating with data teams but also believing and showing actively the positive impact of making decisions rooted in data.

- **Guiding** other leaders and teams to actively go for fact-based decisions, connect with data experts and leaders in the organization, and be both a coach and a mentor in that regard for others.

For example, a Chief Marketing Officer should discuss the importance of data in wider town halls, make conscious data-informed decisions about campaign optimization for specific product categories, and guide the operational marketing teams to work closely with their data and analytics counterparts.

Having data collaboration at the top of the hierarchy creates positive ripple effects on the data, which can only lead to significant improvements in the data culture. It might not be written into the data strategy this way, but it should always be kept in mind by those who manage the data strategy.

Trust is the foundation for collaboration

I want to close this chapter by focusing on trust. Trust is the foundation of good collaboration because people must believe in each other's skills and motivations to make collaboration work.

Trust goes beyond just people because data and system trustworthiness can also significantly impact business processes, for better or worse. However, they all start at the human level.

If I don't believe in the quality of the data that comes out of a system but trust the team responsible for managing the data, it will have a positive spillover effect from the human side to the data and system side.

It also means that we should all continuously measure trustworthiness across people, data, and systems through feedback and surveys because, of all the root causes of bad collaboration, a lack of trust might be at the top of the list.

Trust should be the underlying foundation of data strategy and the outcome of a "humanized" data strategy.

Four

Communication

Data professionals use communication in:

- Explaining complex matters in simple, relatable ways
- Convincing senior stakeholders to get buy-in
- Using diagrams to illustrate structures and visualize challenges
- Describing common goals between different functions
- Writing formal policies and then translating them into technical requirements
- Telling compelling stories about data initiatives and their impact

In the context of data strategy, we need to enable and encourage communication as well as establish platforms and communities for cross-functional communication.

Data strategy always starts with a target state, an understanding of where you are now and a roadmap for how to get there. This means that a data strategy always implies change. And any change requires change management. When we think about changes needed in people, process, and technology, the people aspect of change is truly the hardest but also the most rewarding.

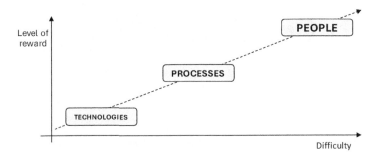

Peter Senge, the famous American systems scientist and senior lecturer at the MIT Sloan School of Management, once said, "People don't resist change, they resist being changed." We need continuous and frequent communication to move from enforcing a data strategy and directives, to turning people into intrinsically motivated and active change advocates.

Framing value on an organizational and personal level

The most important aspect of communicating a data strategy is being clear about its purpose. What are the benefits gained from following the data strategy?

While connecting the data strategy goals to the organization's overarching strategic objectives is important, communicating those is just not enough. The key lies in the framing because what is even more convincing for individual employees than organizational impact is how the strategy helps them individually on a personal level.

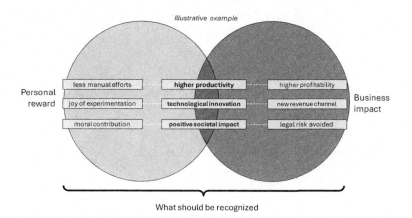

If one of the strategic goals on an organizational level is higher profitability, the common ground between organizational and personal value might be higher productivity. On a personal level, this means that a group of people needs to spend significantly less manual effort on certain data tasks.

Another example could be the goal of establishing a new revenue channel, leading to the common ground of business impact and personal reward being technological innovation, which then tackles the personal reward of the joy of experimentation.

One last illustrative example might be the goal of avoiding legal or regulatory risks, which ties to the common ground of positive societal impact, which, on a personal level, should appeal to achieving a moral contribution.

You can also see the framing of personal reward as making the implications of organizational achievements for individuals more explicit because not everyone can easily connect the dots between strategic goals and personal needs.

Framing at a personal level needs to be done differently for different audiences, indicating that there should not be a one-size-fits-all approach to communicating a data strategy. Instead, any data strategy should have various versions of more nuanced communication plans.

Storytelling narrative for buy-in and reducing resistance

When I was a bar pianist during my university years, I realized that identifying what the guests liked to hear by seeing their reactions to music could make the music I was playing more impactful, and most importantly, I would get more tips from the audience. Having the right content for the right audience is key.

Telling a compelling story to convince stakeholders and collaborators about the importance and necessity of data initiatives in your data strategy can take many shapes, and it all starts with the audience. It's always about the audience's point of view. What does the audience care about? What would convince them to believe in what you're proposing? What are the reasons that they might resist?

Once you understand your audience deeply, one high-level narrative structure is pretty simple: the WHY, the WHAT, and the HOW–exactly in that order. Let's break it down into more detail:

- **The WHY:** Start by understanding your audience and discussing the purpose of the data strategy. Frame it on an organizational and personal level. Give the audience an undeniable reason to care and to pay attention to the data strategy.

- **The WHAT:** Ensure that required decisions, actions, and commitments are explained in a language the audience understands and cannot misinterpret. Be especially specific about the requirements and urgency.

- **The HOW:** Propose an action plan with resources, timeline, and deliverables, co-develop the details with the audience, and commit to the next steps together. Make sure it becomes a shared priority for all priorities in the shape of OKRs, common goals, or other processes that ensure collaboration in the organization.

For example, the WHY of the new data strategy is tied to a business transformation from a B2B to a B2C sales model. The WHAT is about ensuring that data collection, processing, and usage, as well as related business acumen, are adapted to the new business model. The HOW is defining a roadmap, responsibilities, milestones, and overall program management to guide the transformation.

Data professionals are usually incredibly proud of their work, which is usually reflected in talking a lot about the HOW instead of starting with the WHY and the WHAT–but the collective purpose and applied empathy can give the detailed achievements a better framing.

Always communicate the data strategy in this structure. It also works perfectly as a structure for more tactical and operational communication, such as project introductions, product backlog sessions, or even self-introductions to new stakeholders.

The art of using humor for impact

A data analyst, a data scientist, a data engineer, and a data governor go to a bar.

Data analyst: "I want a beer that reaches 90% of the glasses' capacity."

Data scientist: "Make sure my beer is clean. Otherwise, I have to adjust my digestion algorithm."

Data engineer: "Can I have a straw, a spoon, and some swim shorts so I can be flexible on how to access the beer?"

Data governor: "You're all wrong. If you had checked the drink lineage, you'd notice that you're all ordering soda instead of beer. Should have looked into the beer catalog!"

In the end, they all went to a lakehouse and self-served whatever drinks they wanted and called it a "Beer Mesh."

I wrote this joke as a data-themed version of the infamous "x, y, and z go to a bar" joke. I'm especially proud of that joke because it achieves three things: using analogies to show what the different data roles care about when it comes to data, showing the importance of data lineage in data governance, and explaining one of the benefits of the data mesh.

Just because we have to take data work seriously doesn't mean we shouldn't be able to have fun talking and communicating about it. Laughter relieves stress and boredom, increases engagement and well-being, and spurs creativity, collaboration, and productivity.[9]

Telling jokes might not be everybody's cup of tea, but just like creativity or storytelling, humor is also a muscle you can train. I'm a big fan of stand-up comedy and have semi-scientifically tried to understand the magic behind one person selling out stadiums just by telling jokes alone on stage.

Similar to the classical joke structure, there are four parts:

---

[9] https://hbr.org/2014/05/leading-with-humor - visited May 26th, 14:16.

- Premise: Bringing the audience into the environment and context of what will happen next.

- Setup: Preparing with statements that create suspense and anticipation of where the joke will go.

- Punchline: The unexpected surprise that will generate the laugh itself.

- Tags: Additional commentary that adds to the humor of the punchline.

In the beer joke above, the premise was the data people going into a bar, the setup was everyone ordering their drinks, the punchline was data governance telling them none of them ordered actual beer, and the tag was that they could self-serve themselves beer in a beer mesh.

Another easy way to insert humor into your data strategy is using analogies. The benefit of analogies is that they are equally about explaining something complex in a more relatable manner and making it possible to cause joy when applied correctly. Data governance is one of the most difficult to explain data disciplines, so I had to often go back to using analogies. For example, data governance has already been the referee in a football game, the foundation of a tall building, the Jedi council if data was the force—and in specific contexts and for specific audiences, it worked.

Using humor in your communication can make your data strategy more memorable and appeal more to the emotional side of your audience. Most importantly, being able to laugh about your work makes you more charming and approachable. As a data leader, you will also show vulnerability in the day-to-day.

Stakeholder management by identifying personas

Another important reason for communication is managing collaboration with stakeholders and collaborators while planning, executing, or reviewing the data strategy. Communicating well to establish advocacy is important not only for stakeholders in senior leadership but also for collaborating with peers and team members in the data teams. However, not all stakeholders have the same attitudes and behaviors toward data strategy, which is why mapping stakeholders across two dimensions can be a great start to tailoring your communication: active/passive versus detractors/promoters.

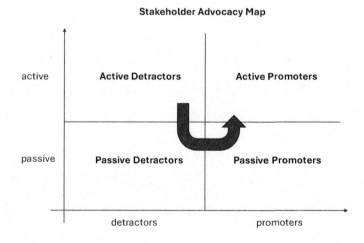

We distribute the stakeholders across four quadrants with different communicative actions to take:

- **Active Detractors:** Stakeholders who are negatively vocal about your data strategy can be destructive. Immediate conversations are required to solve any misunderstandings and to at least limit the negative word of mouth to a certain extent.

- **Passive Detractors:** These passive detractors are quiet because they are most likely skeptical but want to wait and see how the data strategy will pan out. Having some healthy criticism is not necessarily bad, as long as they are not secretly sabotaging data efforts towards the strategic goals. Some regular communication about concrete achievements and progress to address their skepticism could slowly melt the ice.

- **Passive Promoters:** Having buy-in and a positive perception is good, but having stakeholders talk about it proactively is even better. Approach these passive promoters with opportunities to publicly share their positive opinions and contributions towards the data strategy, turning them from passive to active.

- **Active Promoters:** These are the "best friends" of your data strategy. They are already doing a great job actively advocating for your data strategy, so the only thing you can do from a communication point of view is ensure you do not lose them. Keep them happy.

It's impossible to never have any detractors, but it's important to continuously make an effort to turn those detractors into promoters. To make this a more structured approach, it can be helpful to categorize stakeholders even further into more persona types, such as:

- **Thinkers versus Doers:** Some people like to think about everything deeply but are not a big fan of actions, and there are some people who jump to taking actions without thinking it through. Most people are in between these two extremes. Communicating to thinkers and doers requires different balances between theoretical background and actionable implications.

- **Believers versus Skeptics:** People who naturally believe in good intentions and innovation need fewer facts to convince them and are more excited about how to make it happen, whereas skeptics need a lot more convincing with facts and outcomes and a clear acknowledgment of their worries and fears.

- **Givers versus Takers:** Some people are generous in giving advice and helping with actions, whereas others just like to request help and take support for granted. When communicating a data strategy, it's important to manage expectations and clearly illustrate what kind of collaboration is needed.

Communicating with stakeholders requires understanding them. Still, tools, such as persona mapping, introduced in this chapter, can make it easier and more reproducible. This way, communication about data strategy can be tailored to different audiences.

The "action fallacy"

It's just human nature. We all love heroes who save the day but rarely care about the people who ensured that the day never needed saving in the first place. Mitigating issues get more attention and awareness than preventing issues.

From a data risk management point of view, mitigating issues is always more expensive than preventing them. If a data strategy is executed right, especially when data governance is implemented correctly, then most of the issues should have been prevented and not mitigated after the fact.

To ensure more awareness of data issue prevention, we must start with our own mindsets and clearly see prevention as an achievement. The communication of data issue prevention will then follow accordingly, and we can communicate the value of related initiatives in the data strategy.

For example, when there are data quality issues. Getting these quality issues solved once is a clear achievement. However, setting up a monitoring solution with an attached prevention and mitigation process is the follow-up that brings continuous value moving forward.

Mitigating issues is a one-off success, but preventing issues is always a continuous success that can be communicated as success over time.

While issue and incident mitigation are usually known places in data strategy, it's equally important to include issue and incident prevention as well—put together ideally as a holistic "issue management" process. A data strategy should define it as a priority and then communicate it in a way that values both issue mitigation and prevention.

Feedback as a measure of success

When we establish a KPI framework to measure the success of a data strategy, we usually have a set of business performance-related and operational KPIs, all of which help guide the decisions and actions made in data.

However, if we want to take the human aspect of data strategy more seriously, then it should also be reflected in measures of success. Asking for feedback is not only a great measure of communication to nurture collaboration, but setting up feedback-based KPIs can also enable a more regular cadence of asking for feedback and enforce actions in case certain challenges surface from feedback conversations.

Feedback-based KPIs that measure the "human" aspect of data strategy could be:

- **Team Advocacy:** Usually measured for employer branding, asking data team members how likely they would recommend to work in the data team can indicate happiness inside the team, but also how likely talent rotation with business teams can happen.

- **Stakeholder Satisfaction:** It's easy to get wrapped up in the day-to-day collaboration, but asking stakeholders about their satisfaction with the data teams allows us to regularly take a step back to assess the collaboration and what could be further improved.

- **Leadership NPS:** Knowing how senior leaders perceive the strategic efforts with data can help assess the clarity of the communication around data efforts and how to ensure continuous buy-in and sponsorship.

Having feedback-based KPIs also motivates all data professionals to make asking for feedback a habit, an important pillar of a collaboration based on co-creation and trust.

Realistic Optimism versus Toxic Positivity

It's so easy to focus on things that are not working–people love complaining about things. When communicating about data strategy, focusing too strongly on the risks and challenges without acknowledging the achievements can cause a continuous negative perception of data efforts, which can be fatal. There's also the other extreme where all the negative things are ignored and only positive (and often artificially-forced) aspects are mentioned–often referred to as "toxic positivity."

To find balance, communication around data strategy should always apply "realistic optimism"–which means addressing the positive while acknowledging the negative. The underlying logic is that with any unexpected challenges happening, at least they were identified and efforts were made to solve them.

A few examples of realistic optimism are the following:

- Don't say: "I don't know what you're talking about, all our data pipelines are running great." Instead, say: "Thanks for openly telling us about our data pipeline challenges–we wouldn't have been able to address them in this timely manner without your help."

- Don't say: "We didn't see the new regulations coming and now we will have to stop some of our projects." Instead, say: "We are avoiding legal risks by putting these projects on hold, but the good news is that we are putting measures in place, including a closer collaboration with the legal teams to anticipate these risks more in advance."

- Don't say: "The restructuring of the wider organizations is making our data efforts complicated, it's unclear what we need to do for now." Instead, say: "The restructuring is putting more emphasis on the newly defined strategic goals, and it will, after a transition phase, make the efforts of our data work even more impactful."

The good thing about realistic optimism is that it multiplies after sharing it with others. Once everyone has a healthy, balanced mindset about challenges in the data strategy, it will improve the organization's overall culture.

Intentional communication requires planning

All of the previously mentioned topics have one objective in common: being more intentional with communication. In other words, proactively communicating with a purpose instead of reactively communicating when asked.

This is why having a communication plan as part of the data strategy is important—to have a systematic and tactical approach to address different topics to different audiences in different ways.

A communication toolbox helps you to predefine key aspects of your communication so you can have a structured approach to plan your communication upfront, as follows:

- **Target:** Define the key audiences you want to communicate to and segment them with the previously mentioned techniques, such as persona-based, to be able to address them with different messages.

- **Topic:** Define the topics you want to discuss–and find a balance between operational, tactical, and strategic messages. Talking about project updates requires a different type of communication than giving an inspirational keynote on the new data strategy.

- **Channel:** Define your key communication channels based on the target audience's preference and how tailored your messaging and engagement needs to be. A one-on-one meeting is far more effective than an email newsletter in getting a tailored message across. Always balance personal communication in smaller groups with wider public communication.

- **Frequency:** Define how often your message and engagement need to go out. Not everything needs to be of the highest frequency. Despite planning out frequencies for communication, it's important to leave enough flexibility for ad-hoc communication. There are always unexpected things worth communicating, both good and bad.

- **Responsible:** Communication in a data strategy should not always come from the same people. Divide and conquer different communication based on relationships with the target audience and stakeholders. Also, it's an opportunity to allow more junior team members to practice their communication skills.

Once you have defined all that, you can visualize it in a toolbox, as depicted below.

Communication Toolbox
(with example communication path)

TARGET	TOPIC	CHANNEL	FREQUENCY	RESPONSIBLE
Senior Leader	Strategic Progress	E-Mail	Daily	Chief Data Officer
Tech & IT	Collaboration Stories	Chat	Weekly	Head of Data Engineering
Business Functions	Request for Feedback	Meeting	Bi-Weekly	Head of Data Governance
Wider Public	Team Recognition	Webinar	Monthly	Head of Data Science
...	...	...	...	...

You can see all your defined choices at a glance and visualize your choices for specific communication measures in a path from left to right. These choices can now be reflected in content planning, such as pre-writing newsletter texts, creating meeting agendas, or outlining webinar topics.

We want any data strategy related communication to be precise, understandable, and memorable, and one key skill needed to make that happen is creativity. Let's talk about that in the next chapter.

Five

Creativity

When I released a rap song about data governance called "Governors of Data,"[10] it made quite a splash within my organization and across the data management community. I believe that happened because of two reasons:

- Nobody made a rap song about data governance before.
- Data people are not perceived as creative.

Now, that sounds a little harsh, but as a born optimist I see a huge potential: every bit of creativity in the data space can leverage the element of surprise to catch attention.

Creativity is usually associated with art and not with analytical jobs. But I believe that those two worlds are not

---

[10] https://youtu.be/EdOzZJd8DNk.

83

too far apart. Let's look, for example, into what music and data have in common.

MUSIC	DATA
DEFINED SCALE OF NOTES	DEFINED SET OF DATA VALUES
TURNING NOTES & SOUNDS INTO ART	TURNING DATA POINTS INTO DATA SETS
EXPRESSING EMOTIONS THROUGH SOUND	EXPRESSING INSIGHTS THROUGH STORIES
PLAYING & LISTENING AS A GROUP	DATA & BUSINESS EXPERTISE IN COLLABORATION
DIFFERENT TASTES IN MUSIC	DIFFERENT REQUIREMENTS TOWARDS DATA

It's all a matter of perspective. You can see art from a mechanical and scientific angle as much as you can see data from a creative and innovative angle, which means creativity is always applicable–as long as we want to.

Creativity is a muscle to train and apply every day. From an organizational point of view, creativity is the underlying human skill required to innovate and stay competitive, and it's needed to remove any existing stigmas around data teams. So, in this chapter, let's apply creativity conceptually and practically in a data strategy.

Not all creativity is the same

Before we get into how to enable practical creativity in your data strategy, it's important to clarify that not all creativity is the same and that there are different types and occasions to be creative:

- **Spontaneous versus solution-oriented creativity:** Spontaneous creativity is the "spark of an idea" often associated with art. It's mostly proactive. For example, an unexpected association between two previously unlinked topics, such as a mindful approach to stakeholder interactions. However, solution-oriented creativity is often an outcome of trying to solve a problem, and it's usually more reactive—for example, finding a way to optimize existing processes.

- **Incremental versus disruptive creativity:** Incremental creativity is heavily reliant on something existing. For example, it might involve writing a meeting summary or making a joke based on a real-life situation. Disruptive creativity, on the other hand, involves an element of absolute newness, such as inventing the wheel.

These two dimensions of creativity mean there are different ways to be creative, and we can map different opportunities and techniques along these two dimensions into a matrix.

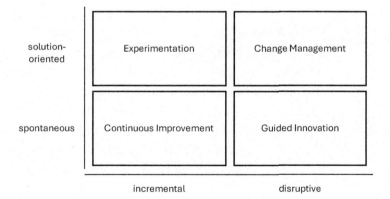

In this two-by-two matrix, we get the four combinations of the two dimensions as follows:

- **Experimentation** is solution-oriented and incremental, whereas, in a controlled environment, solutions with slightly different properties are tested to see which leads to the best outcome. For example, this could be done through website A/B testing.

- **Continuous improvement** is also incremental but takes a more spontaneous approach. Based on unexpected new findings and feedback, small changes lead to a slightly more optimized outcome. For example, this could be redesigning a data catalog starting page based on changing needs.

- **Change Management** is needed when it's solution-oriented but disruptive because a bigger change also requires a more coordinated approach to have synchronized and sustained change. For example, this could be the migration to a new data platform due to new requirements that the old platform cannot meet.

- **Guided innovation** is the answer to having disruptive creativity from a spontaneous place because of its spontaneous nature. This innovation requires more guidance in the shape of sponsorship and funding needed while linking it to business value. For example, this could be the tracking of a first-ever NFT sales activity (although NFTs are at the point of the release of this book probably not as relevant anymore, but you get the gist).

From a data strategy point of view, we should welcome creativity—but by zooming in on those four combinations, a data strategy needs to enable the right environment for creativity to be natural and for creativity to be converted into practical outcomes.

Creating the environment for creativity

Picasso once said, "The enemy of creativity is common sense." And it's true—being creative can feel awkward because it's different than doing what you're used to and what you already know that you're good at. But it's also against common sense because common sense tells you by default that being creative could fail.

But what exactly are the consequences of failing after expressing creativity? I started writing songs when I was 15 and shared a song about my teenage angst of being lonely with all of my classmates—it tanked. My friends were confused and my classmates made fun of me writing songs about "my feelings." But having gone through that, I realized it wasn't that bad. In fact, it made me more resilient towards failure because I realized that this is the worst that could happen. It might sound cheesy, but often, failures are not as severe as we think. They actually help us learn from our mistakes and do our jobs better than we would have without having failed.

From a data strategy point of view, we need to create the right environment so nobody is afraid of failure. With the right balance of guidance and proactive ideas, we can truly leverage people's creativity as a source of innovation. The key ingredient to make this environment work is psychological safety. People should feel comfortable having ideas, putting them into action, and not being punished when some of them inevitably fail.

Applying the previous chapters' collaboration and communication principles can help with that. Still, it also takes proactive, careful interactions with everyone involved in data efforts to feel comfortable about being creative.

So when data team members finally feel good about the answer to "What's the worst that can happen?" in terms of creativity, it's time to encourage everyone to be creative. Data strategy requires innovation, and leveraging everyone's creativity can be a great source to drive innovation effectively and efficiently.

Creativity as a muscle

I truly believe that everyone has creativity in them. Our education and the nature of our professions might have shown us otherwise, but it's one of our core human skills. So, I'd rather see creativity as a muscle. Some of us have trained that muscle more, some less. But as with muscles in our bodies, the key to be good at creativity is to start training it, and never stop continuing to do so.

As data leaders, we need to tackle creativity in three aspects: mindset, practice, and habit. Let me elaborate:

- **Mindset:** First, we need to emphasize that creativity is encouraged and needed for a data strategy to succeed. It's also important to make sure that not every idea needs to be successful and that true innovation lies in failing on the way.

- **Practice:** We then need to allow people to practice their creativity and proactively assign them to team members to collaborate on as a vote of confidence.

- **Habit:** When creativity finally becomes the new default, it's important to protect that culture of ideation and experimentation so it can sustain through a positive environment.

The most important thing about creativity is not just talking about it with big fluffy words but cascading down actions and encouragements through meaningful interactions with all team members and contributors.

Most of our education focuses on memorizing things and passing tests, but we must invest our time and energy into original and unconventional human thinking. When defining and executing a data strategy, we need to empower uniqueness, embrace human interactions, and practice divergent thinking.

Reflection as a source for inspiration

We don't need to wait for the next big crisis to apply creativity. On the contrary, getting started on something with less stakes is probably smarter because the pressure of applying something new to an urgent topic might not be the best combination.

To get started, we should identify anything in our daily lives that could be improved. This is how we can apply creativity in smaller doses. It could be an updated daily routine, a changed communication style with a stakeholder, or trying out a more efficient command in SQL. By reflecting deeply and thoroughly, we can improve even the most mundane tasks.

Reflections are not completely new to working with data, such as having team retrospectives in projects or feedback sessions among peers. So there is a lot of opportunity to reflect and identify areas for improvement.

The higher the dissatisfaction and urgency, the more motivation for change there is–this is where creativity can be a game changer.

Just like creativity is a muscle to help innovate, our conscience should be applied more to critically evaluate the things we do in and with data, and like with creativity, conscience is everyone's responsibility.

Six

Conscience

We live in a world where data is the key to many innovative, cutting-edge things. There are so many exciting things to do with data that we often don't think about taking a step back to evaluate if we are even supposed to do this from an ethical, compliance, and legal point of view.

Following the rules is one approach, but from a data strategy point of view, we should appeal more to the conscience of everyone to be more proactively motivated to not do anything wrong and activate people's human judgment.

Human judgment is recognizing relationships, drawing conclusions from evidence, and evaluating events and people. In other words, human beings have the talent to evaluate right versus wrong, good versus bad, and ethical versus unethical.

Having this moral compass is a natural instinct, but it is not stable and has evolved over time–and that's a good thing! Otherwise, we'd probably still condone slavery, colonialism, and torture. But it also means that we cannot just trust technologies and algorithms to imitate human judgment because it won't change for the better without human interference and oversight.

If we don't use our judgment for the good, then bad things can and will happen: data leaks, biased AI models, and targeted scam bots are only the beginning.

We need to empower human judgment in our data strategies and continuously listen to the voices of concern and reason to avoid risks of bad actions–actions that we might never recover from. We talked about the difference between "data-driven" and "data-informed." Our conscience ringing alarm bells means we should do the latter more than the former. Let's talk about how to make it happen.

Optimism as a motivator for positive change

How many optimists does it take to change a light bulb?

None, because they always see light in the darkness.

Now that I made you chuckle (or let out a small air breeze through your nostrils), I hope I counteracted the pretty pessimistic introduction to this chapter with a little humor.

Optimism is the tendency to expect good things in the future. But when you expect good things, you can face it in two ways: either passively, where you just sit back and wait for the good thing to happen, or actively, where you do everything in your power to increase the likelihood of a good outcome.

In psychology, this attitude and activism toward a better future is also described as psychological capital,[11] which includes three more elements besides optimism:

- Hope, which means persevering towards goals

- Resilience, which means sustaining when faced with problems and adversity, and

- Self efficacy, which means having the confidence to succeed at challenging tasks

Sitting back and hoping that doing anything with data will have a good outcome is not enough. We need to enable psychological capital for everyone involved in the planning and operationalization of data strategy to be active optimists willing to work towards the best possible outcome of data efforts and not lose that motivation when faced with setbacks–by applying their conscience and human judgment.

The number of actions we can take to apply our human judgment is closely connected with the expertise that exists to make positive changes in data, which means that optimism has to go hand in hand with increased data

---

[11] https://doi.org/10.1016/j.orgdyn.2020.100817.

literacy. For example, if we want to actively ensure that customer data is not being leaked to criminals to scam them, we need to understand what preventative measures we can take—before something bad happens.

Creating the right environment for all data contributors to be actively optimistic is key, and using the right language and communication styles in a data strategy plays a huge part in it.

The four types of data concerns

There can be lots of concerns around data risks where human judgment is needed, but we can cluster the most prominent ones that can have serious societal damage into four types:

- **Data privacy concerns:** Ensuring that personally identifiable information (PII) is managed securely and ethically. For example, we should ensure that email addresses and phone numbers are not widely shared within an organization.

- **Data security concerns:** Ensuring that sensitive information is not leaked or accessed in an unauthorized way, especially when there's malicious intent. For example, we should not allow everyone access to current financial data to avoid insider trading.

- **Data ethics concerns:** Ensuring that data is being used ethically where there are no definitive disadvantages to specific groups of people. For example, we should ensure that women are not underrepresented in our defined customer segments.

- **Ungoverned AI:** Ensuring that AI models are trained with unbiased and fair data, and that the models themselves are explained and not causing any type of risk for the organization, customers, or society. For example, we should ensure that people of color are not more often associated with crime in a generative AI use case.

As established before, forcing these concerns without context on data strategy contributors can be quite the endeavor, so it's important to motivate them intrinsically. For those concerns, the key is to appeal to everyone's empathy: "How would you feel if your confidential data was mismanaged?"

It's easy to see data as a pile of anonymous and lifeless tables of numbers and text. Still, since we want to use it to drive value in a data strategy, the opposite is true. So, we should treat data with the necessary respect, diligence, and care.

Defining a data strategy roadmap that regularly captures all data concerns with key stakeholders in organizations can be a great way to assess what concerns are being addressed, but it also puts thinking empathetically about these concerns top of mind again.

Cross-functional oversight empowers the conscience

Besides appealing to the empathy of everyone involved, there needs to be a formal call to action to take these concerns seriously and a way to enforce the prevention and mitigation of those risks. Cross-functional decision-making bodies such as committees and steering boards can help with that. In most cases, these decision-making bodies that focus on data topics already exist, and we can leverage them to drive the application of human judgment and critical thinking in the right way. Here are some typical decision-making bodies that we can build upon:

- **Data Governance Committee:** A group of data owners and stewards deciding what data policies must be established and enforced. This group does not have to only focus on commercial objectives–ethical and legal topics should also be thoroughly discussed and agreed upon here.

- **Enterprise Architecture Group:** Usually, a group of different enterprise architects governs any type of architectural changes at the business, data, application, or technology level. On the business and data level, a more human-focused view can be further infused.

- **AI Governance Committee:** Admittedly, AI governance is a relatively new topic at the time of writing this book, but nonetheless, I see this topic growing more important as the number of failures and risks attached to AI applications grows. Like data governance, which focuses on data objects and relationships, AI governance will focus on AI models and their interactions and data machines. Human oversight is especially critical here because I don't believe we have, as a whole, yet thought about all the negative consequences that could result from applying certain new AI models.

The ethical and moral aspects in these groups will become increasingly important, and having the right point of view is important, especially when it comes to a difficult-to-define aspect such as ethics. When in doubt, it is better to have more voices of reason represented than too few because the consequences might be irreversible.

Diversity, Equity, and Inclusion in data

We data people love to talk about how awesome it is to work in data. By doing so, we often create the notion that working in data is very complicated and difficult, which unfortunately creates a barrier of entry for many interested in data but have not started with it yet.

While diversity, equity, and inclusion (DEI) have become increasingly important, especially in larger corporations, I think the same needs to be applied specifically to data. If we want true, equal, co-creative collaboration with business expert peers, we need to remove the fear or bias towards data and make data a more inclusive space. It all comes down to active efforts to demystify the difficulties around data and encourage people just to get started.

Ironically, we could learn from the data itself–isn't data itself always diverse and everchanging? If we try to make sense of all the data at any given time, shouldn't we ensure the right people are there to do it together? The heads and hearts are important, but in this critical matter, so are the voices. Providing feedback to avoid doing wrong things with data is not only an option. It is our duty.

We need to have diverse points of view and experiences in our data disciplines, ensure that data practices and programs provide equal possible entries and outcomes for everyone, and create a sense of belonging in data efforts for data experts and non-experts alike.

DEI should play a strong role in the people aspect of any data strategy. A good starting point could be just to create communities of trust that could be openly endorsed by data leadership, such as "Women in data" or "Asians in data engineering".

Keeping data sustainable for a better world

We're all trying to slow global warming down and save the world for our children and all generations after that. Data plays an important role in this for two reasons: 1) We can use data to make more fact-based decisions that focus on reducing the carbon footprint, and 2) Data work itself creates a carbon footprint that should be kept to a minimum.

Organizations need to make money to keep growing, and some ways of doing that might directly conflict with sustainability-related efforts. However, commercial and sustainability goals should not be kept separately, and the trade-off should be a key aspect of prioritizing or deprioritizing certain programs and projects. Data can help quantify the commercial impact (e.g., revenue) and the sustainability impact (e.g., carbon footprint).

Even more, data can generally help to make existing processes more sustainable through various use cases, such as:

- Optimizing resource usage
- Reducing waste
- Energy efficiency
- Sustainable urban planning
- Environmental monitoring and protecting
- Corporate sustainability reporting

But data itself has a carbon footprint in any organization as well, so when we make decisions on how to set up our data infrastructure, we need to consider the environmental and sustainability angle as well:

- Data centers consume significant amounts of electricity
- Network infrastructure contributes to energy consumption

- Device usage of computers and smartphones consumes energy
- Computing big data requires processing power

We need to ensure that we can use data to make better and more sustainable decisions and manage data in the most sustainable way possible. There is no better way to do that than starting by making this a goal in a data strategy.

SEVEN

Putting it into Action

Congratulations on making it almost to the end of this book. I hope you enjoyed all the impulses to focus more on the human aspect of data strategy. To make it even more actionable, here is a questionnaire that you can use to reflect and assess how "human-centric" your data strategy currently is.

Competence:
- How well is your data literacy program tailored to your organization and the different business domains?

- How well are you supporting the data team members to gain business acumen?

- How well are you creating opportunities to practice and apply what they have learned?

- How well are you enabling an academy-like concept to drive module-based learning, group learning experiences, learning rewards, and communities of practice?

- How well are you creating leadership opportunities and assessing people's leadership skills separate from their practitioner skills?

- How well have you established processes for career progression and job rotations?

- How well are your "guiding principles" defined to encourage the right mindsets and behaviors in learning, growing, and leading?

Collaboration:
- How well are you embedding collaboration skills into the talent lifecycle?

- How well are you encouraging collaboration through transparency and human interactions?

- How well are you encouraging co-creation as a way of collaboration?

- How well are you connecting data roles along the data lifecycle?

- How well are you applying the "follow the pain" approach?

- How well are you applying the concept of finding your "data purpose"?

- How well are you applying "Think big, but start small" into your strategic roadmap?

- How well are you balancing ad-hoc requests to planned data efforts?

- How well are you establishing a positive mindset towards success in the data team?

- How well have you established communities of practice around data?

- How well is your data culture role modeled by senior leaders?

- How high is the trust towards the data and data team in your organization?

Communication:
- How well are you framing the value of data on an organizational and personal level?

- How well are you applying the why-what-how structure to your data strategy narrative?

- How well have you mapped your stakeholders towards different personas?

- How well are you communicating issue prevention as an achievement?

- How well are you measuring feedback as an outcome of your communication?

- How well are you applying realistic optimism when discussing negative topics?

- How well have you established a communication plan in your data strategy?

Creativity:
- How well are you enabling experimentation, continuous improvement, change management, and guided innovation in your data strategy?

- How well is the psychological safety and culture in your team to encourage creativity?

- How well are we enabling mindset, practice, and habits of creativity in our data efforts?

- How well are reflections used for creative inspiration in your data teams?

Conscience:
- How well is active optimism encouraged in your data organization?

- How well are data concerns addressed in an empathetic way?

- How well are ethical elements addressed in your decision-making bodies?

- How well is DEI established as a key focus in your data strategy?

- How well is sustainability established as a key focus in your data strategy?

You can use this questionnaire in many ways: alone, in groups, or in workshops. What is most impactful is that answering these questions can lead to actual improvement actions.

Here's a suggestion how you could do it:

- **As-is assessment**: Use the questionnaire to honestly evaluate how "human-centric" your data strategy is. Identify the strengths and weaknesses.

- **To-be definition:** Define where you want to be with your data strategy at any given time. The goal is to build on existing strengths and to mitigate weaknesses.

- **Roadmap creation:** Based on the as-is and the to-be, you can define what actions to take on a timeline. Make sure to have continuous assessment checkpoints to measure progress in between.

I shouldn't have to say this, but many of the things written in this book are not that ground-breaking. In fact, they should all feel completely natural because they're rooted in human empathy and the natural need for purpose. So, if you already feel inspired to act immediately, don't let this comprehensive gap analysis approach above stop you from taking incremental, quick actions to improve your data efforts.

The goal of humanizing your data strategy is always about doing better. And we can always do better, especially when it's about working with and for people.

Closing Words

This book has provided various impulses about how to humanize data strategy, so let's close this book with a few final thoughts to hopefully provoke your further thinking:

- **Technology should support and not replace humanity.** It's amazing what today's opportunities of AI and automation are capable of, but these can and should not replace human beings in any way. It should help us save time by automating the manual recurring and tedious tasks, but it should not replace our thinking and human interactions.

- **Working in data is not only exciting, it also comes with responsibility.** How we interact and collaborate around data now will set precedence long into the future. We need to critically review, judge, and provide feedback to take the right actions. AI is learning from human behavior reflected in data, so if we don't act properly now, the wrong behavior will be amplified by machines.

- **Data should be taken seriously, but we can still have fun working with it.** There is a difference between having fun with data and making fun of data. Just because it's a serious topic, we can still have fun while doing it, and we should–because with a humanized data strategy, everyone should be passionate about data and enjoy working with it!

The future of data is in all of our (human) hands. Good luck.

Index

Printed in Great Britain
by Amazon

57426223R00069